Great Hair

by Liza Charlesworth

No part of this publication can be reproduced in whole or in part, or stored in a retrieval system, or transmitted in any form or by any means, electronic, mechanical, photocopying, recording, or otherwise, without written permission of the publisher. For permission, write to Scholastic Inc., 557 Broadway, New York, NY 10012.

ISBN: 978-0-545-25629-2

Illustrated by Anne Kennedy
Designed by Maria Lilja • Colored by Ka-Yeon Kim-Li
Copyright © 2010 by Liza Charlesworth

All rights reserved. Published by Scholastic Inc. Printed in China.

She has long hair.

He has short hair.

She has dark hair.

He has light hair.

She has curly hair.

He has straight hair.

But all these kids
have really great hair!